The C.M. RUSSELL

POSTCARD BOOK

Featuring twenty-two images by Charles Marion Russell
from the permanent collection of the C. M. Russell Museum,
Great Falls, Montana

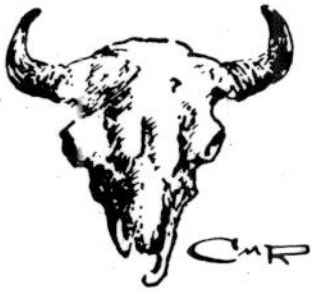

FALCON®
Helena, Montana

A · TWODOT · BOOK

Published in cooperation with the C. M. Russell Museum, 400 Thirteenth Street North, Great Falls, Montana 59401-1498; phone—406-727-8787; fax—406-727-2402. All images in this postcard book are drawn from the permanent collection of the C. M. Russell Museum with the exception of *Lone Wolf,* which is on loan to the Museum from the Jack Hoover Collection.

Design, typesetting, and other composition work by Falcon® Publishing, Inc., Helena, Montana. Printed in Korea.

ISBN 1-56044-358-8

Falcon Press publishes a wide variety of books and calendars. For a free catalog write Falcon Press, P.O. Box 1718, Helena, Montana 59624, or call toll-free 1-800-582-2665.

Front cover: The Fireboat, oil on board, 1918.

THESE SLIGHTLY OVERSIZED POSTCARDS REQUIRE FIRST-CLASS POSTAGE.

FOREWORD

Charles Marion Russell was many things: consummate westerner, historian, advocate of the Northern Plains Indians, cowboy, outdoorsman, writer, philosopher, environmentalist and conservationist, and not least, artist. Born in St. Louis in 1864, he came to the Judith Basin of Montana in 1880 a few days after his sixteenth birthday.

After working for eleven years as a cowboy and wrangler, Russell retired to become a full-time artist, settling with his wife Nancy in Great Falls, Montana. Painting and sculpting in his log cabin studio next to their home, he depicted the scenes of the Old West of which he was so fond. Besides his experiences as a cowboy, he drew upon his friendships with Native Americans, especially the Blood Indians of Alberta, Canada, with whom he spent the summer of 1888. He painted in a time when there was considerable interest in the West, and his work was popular because of its narrative subject matter, unique style, dynamic action, and accuracy.

One of the most widely recognized and distinguished western painters of all time, C. M. Russell completed approximately 4,000 works of art during his lifetime. He knew his subject matter intimately, and he set the standard for the many western artists who followed.

This beautiful postcard book—featuring twenty-two of the most popular Russell works in the permanent collection of the C. M. Russell Museum—celebrates a master's spirit and vision. Enjoy!

LORNE RENDER
Executive Director
C. M. Russell Museum
Great Falls, Montana

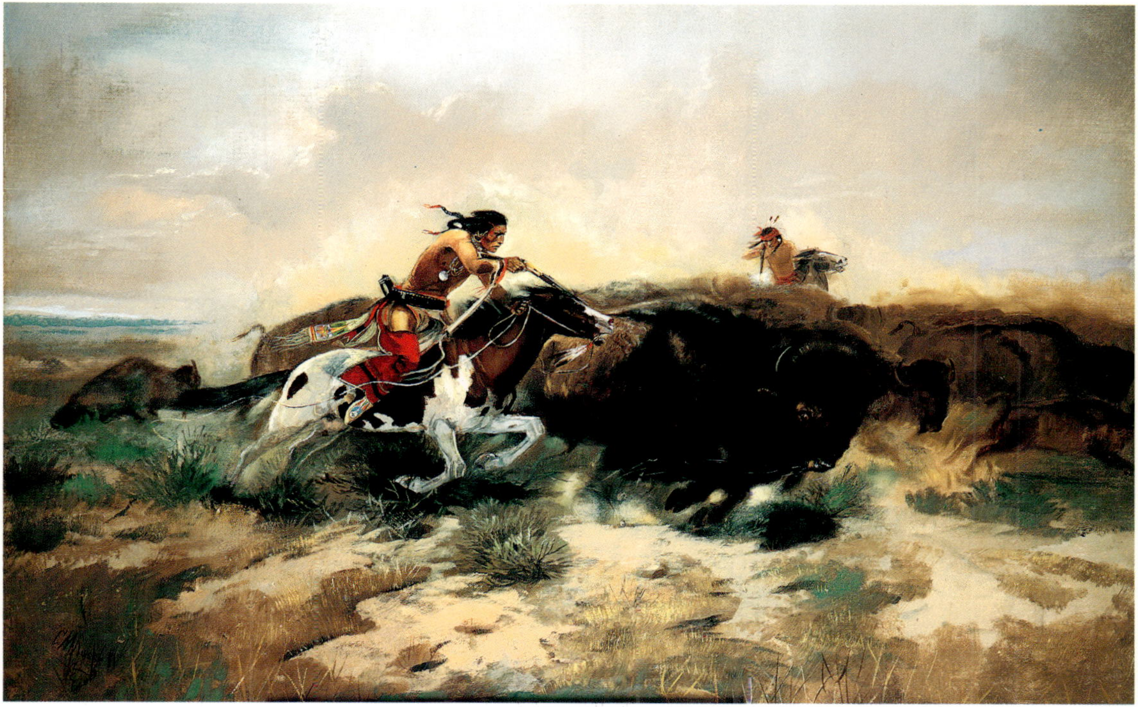

THE C.M. RUSSELL POSTCARD BOOK
Buffalo Hunt, oil, ca. 1890

Charlie Russell came west just as the great buffalo herds were being eradicated, and the bison became a favorite subject. This oil depicts a buffalo hunt in Montana's Judith Basin.

From the collection of the C. M. Russell Museum, Great Falls, MT.

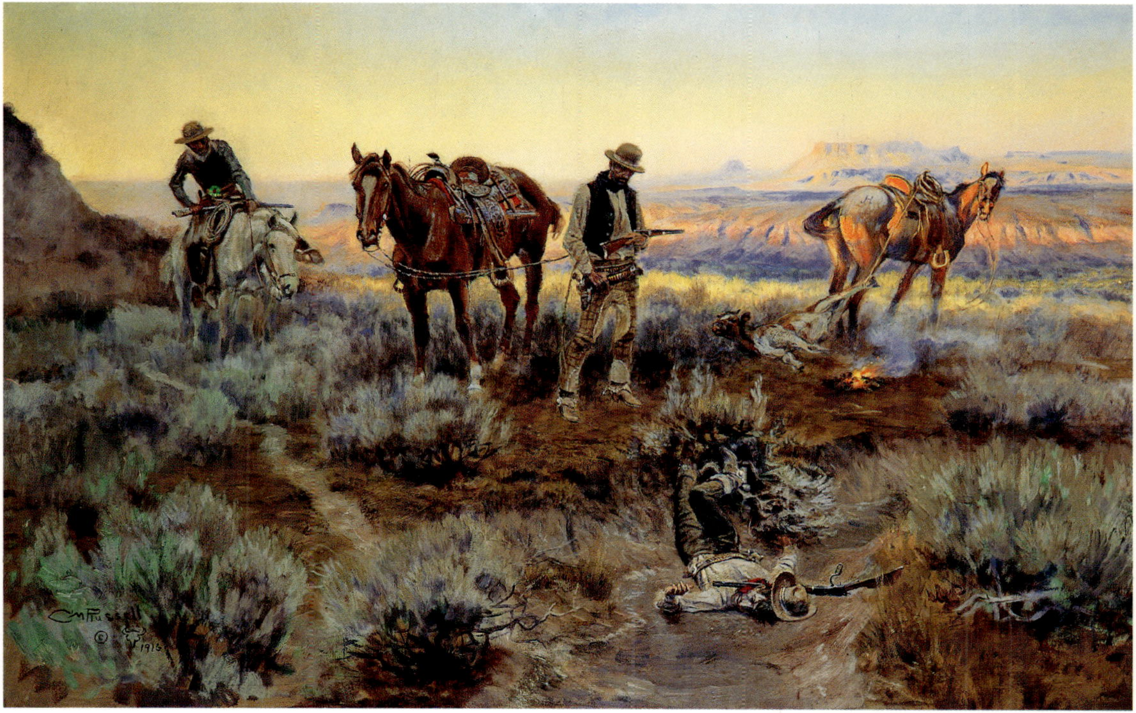
CMRussell
© 1916

Paying the Fiddler, oil, 1916

In this dramatic work, painted at the peak of his career, Russell depicts what could happen when a cattle rustler was caught in the act.

From the collection of the C. M. Russell Museum, Great Falls, MT.

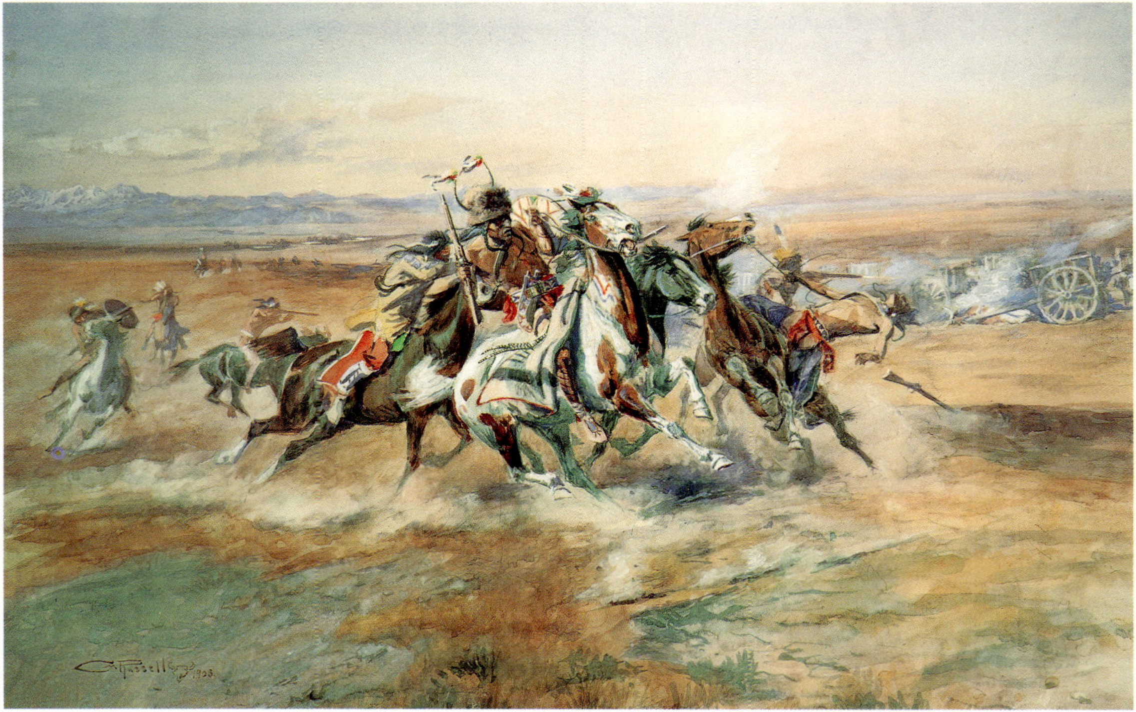

THE C.M. RUSSELL POSTCARD BOOK

Attack on the Red River Carts, watercolor, 1903

This watercolor portrays an attack by Native Americans on the Red River carts of the Metis or mixed-blood people of the northern plains. The Metis were most often of mixed French and American Indian ancestry.

From the collection of the C. M. Russell Museum, Great Falls, MT.

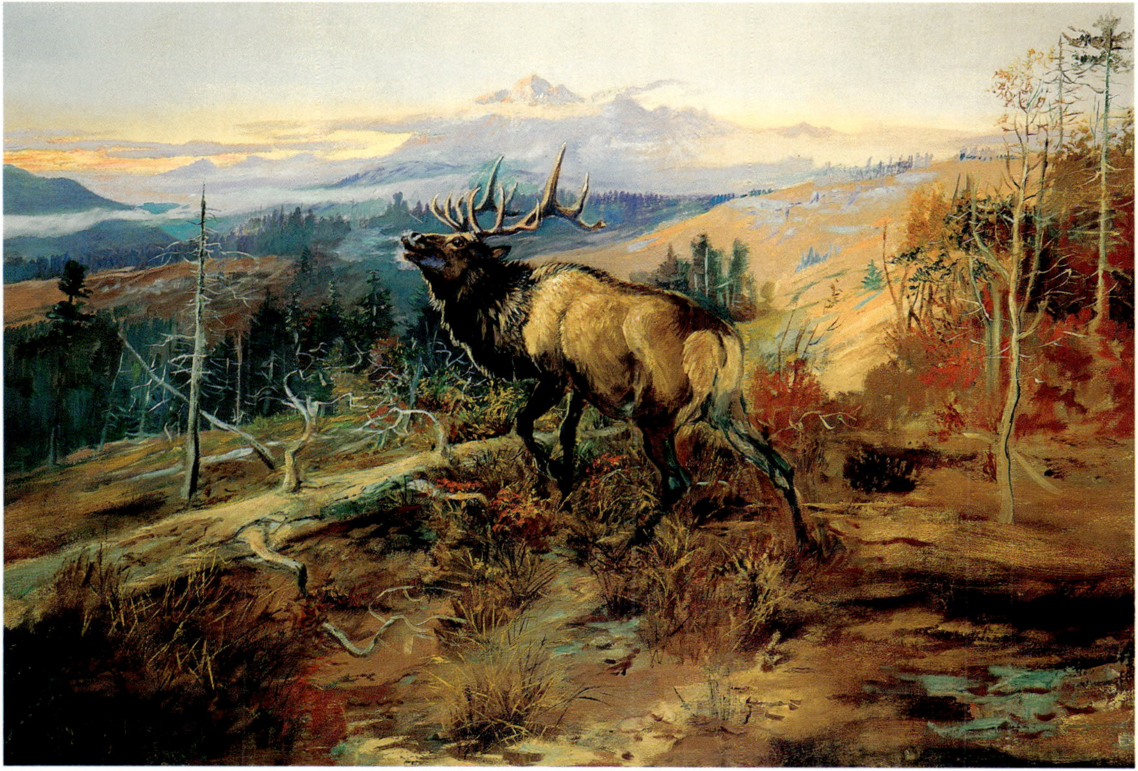

THE C.M. RUSSELL POSTCARD BOOK

The Elk, oil, 1900

From the collection of the C. M. Russell Museum, Great Falls, MT.

Also known as *Monarch of the Forest*, this large oil reveals Russell's considerable skill as a painter of landscapes and animals. He held all wild creatures in high esteem.

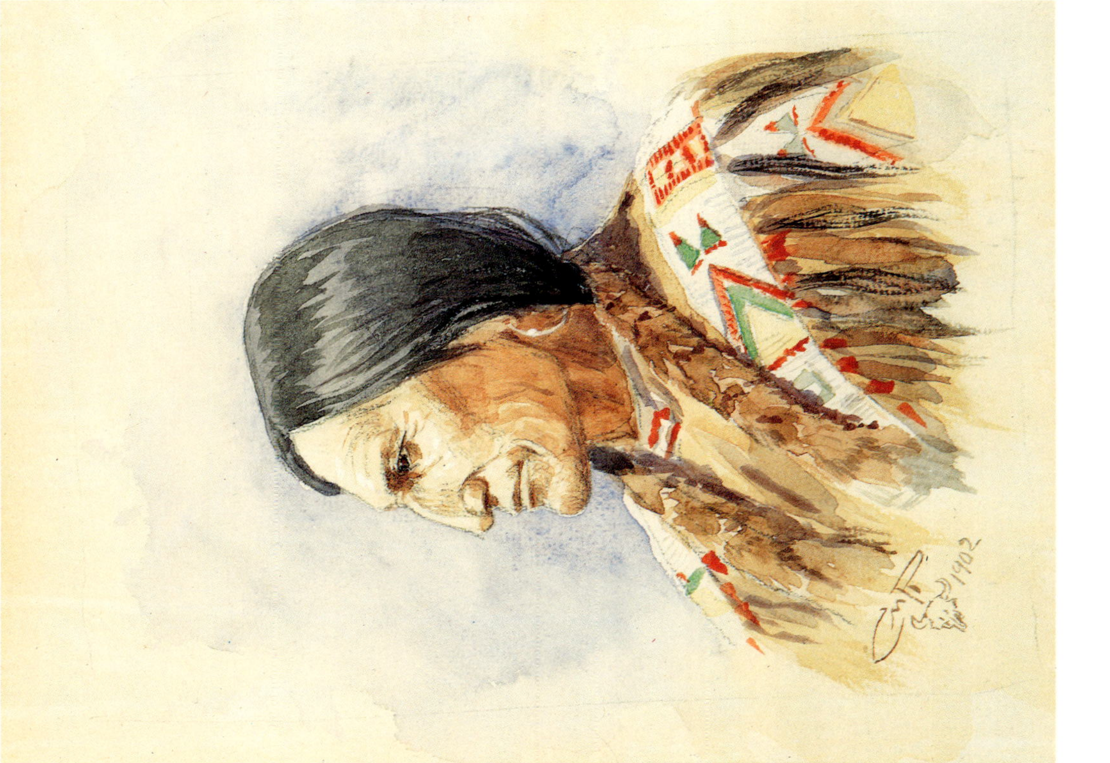
1902

THE C.M. RUSSELL POSTCARD BOOK

Indian Chief, watercolor, 1902

From the collection of the C. M. Russell Museum, Great Falls, MT.

Russell had many friends among the Indian tribes of Montana and Alberta and often portrayed them in vivid detail. His representations of Indian clothing are very accurate.

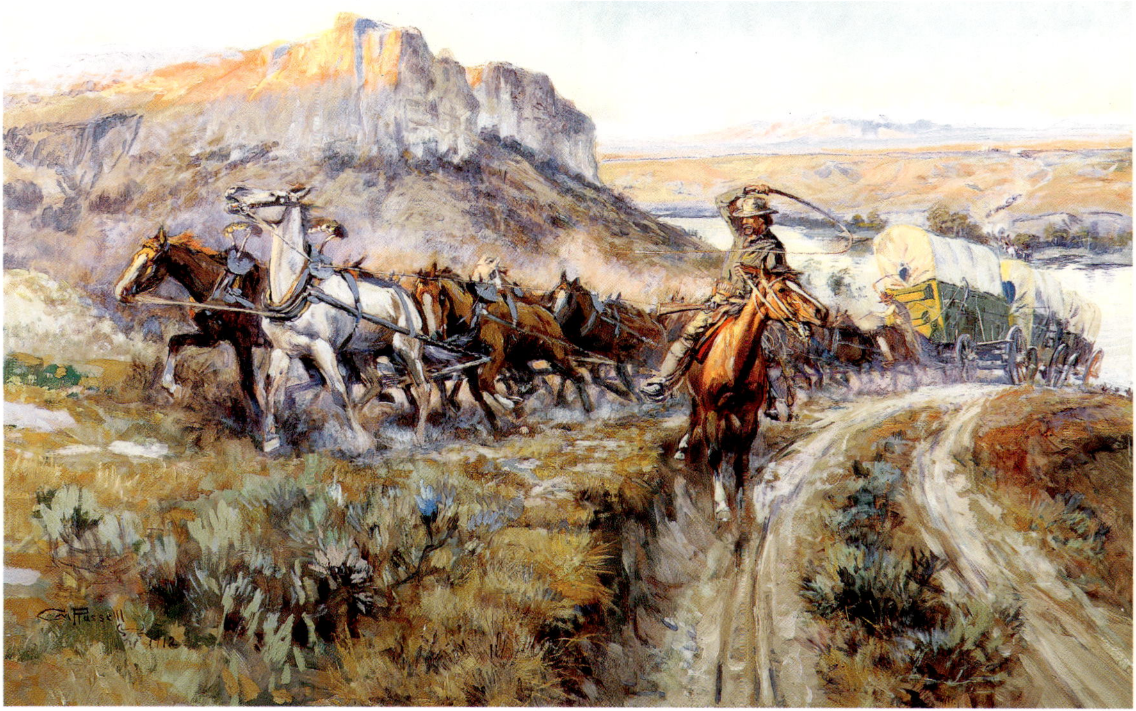
CM Russell
1912

The Jerkline, oil, 1912

This powerful painting–among Russell's best known–depicts a freight team pulling wagonloads of goods up the hill from the Missouri River near Fort Benton, Montana.

From the collection of the C. M. Russell Museum, Great Falls, MT.

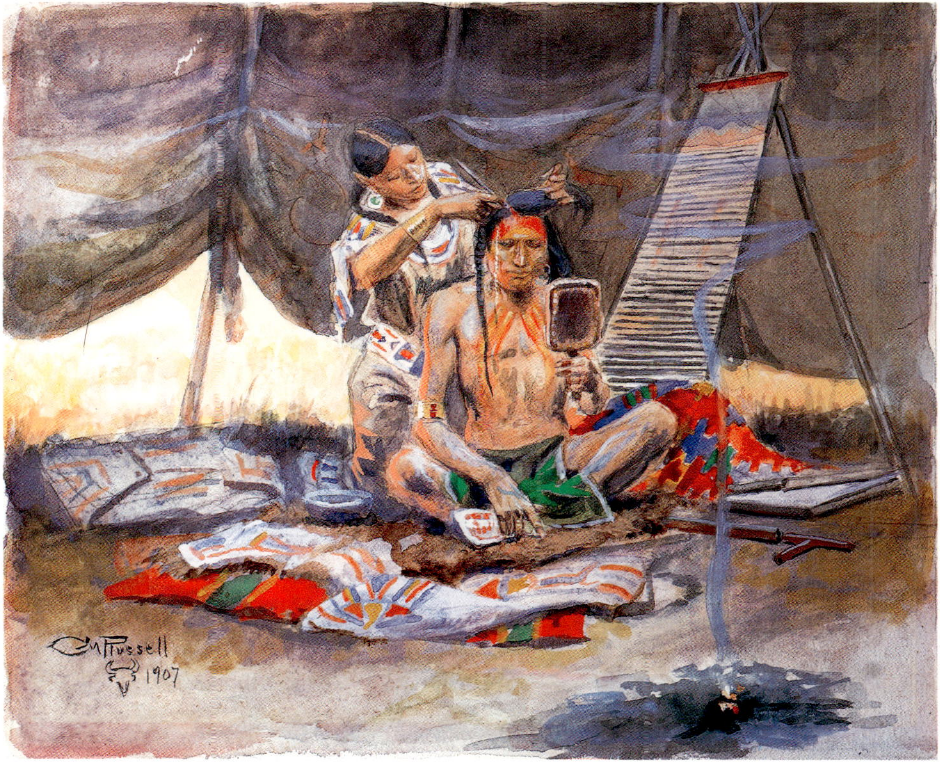
CMRussell
1907

Beauty Parlor, watercolor, 1907

From the collection of the C. M. Russell Museum, Great Falls, MT.

This watercolor reveals the domestic side of Native American culture, providing an opportunity to see such features of a teepee's interior as a back rest, blankets, a pipe, and a parfleche bag.

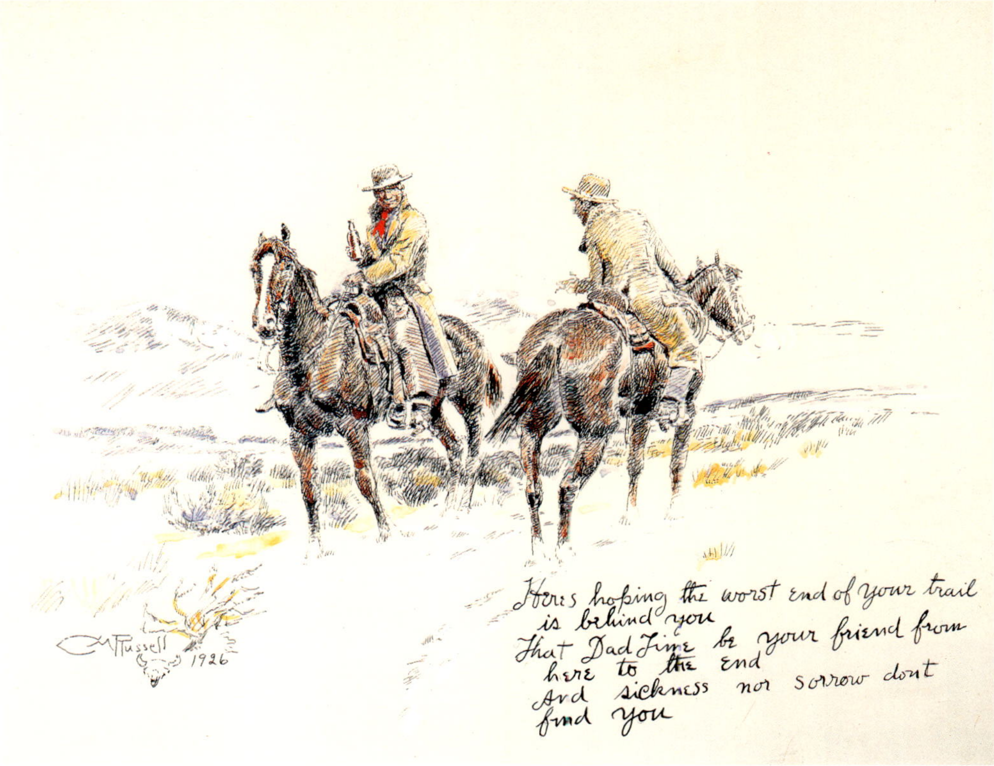
CMRussell
1926
Heres hoping the worst end of your trail
is behind you
That Dad Time be your friend from
here to the end
And sickness nor sorrow dont
find you

THE C.M. RUSSELL POSTCARD BOOK

Here's Hoping the Worst End of Your Trail Is Behind You

watercolor/illustrated poem, 1926

From the collection of the C. M. Russell Museum, Great Falls, MT.

Russell was famous for his illustrated letters and cards. This was his last Christmas card, and in fact, his wife Nancy mailed it after his death.

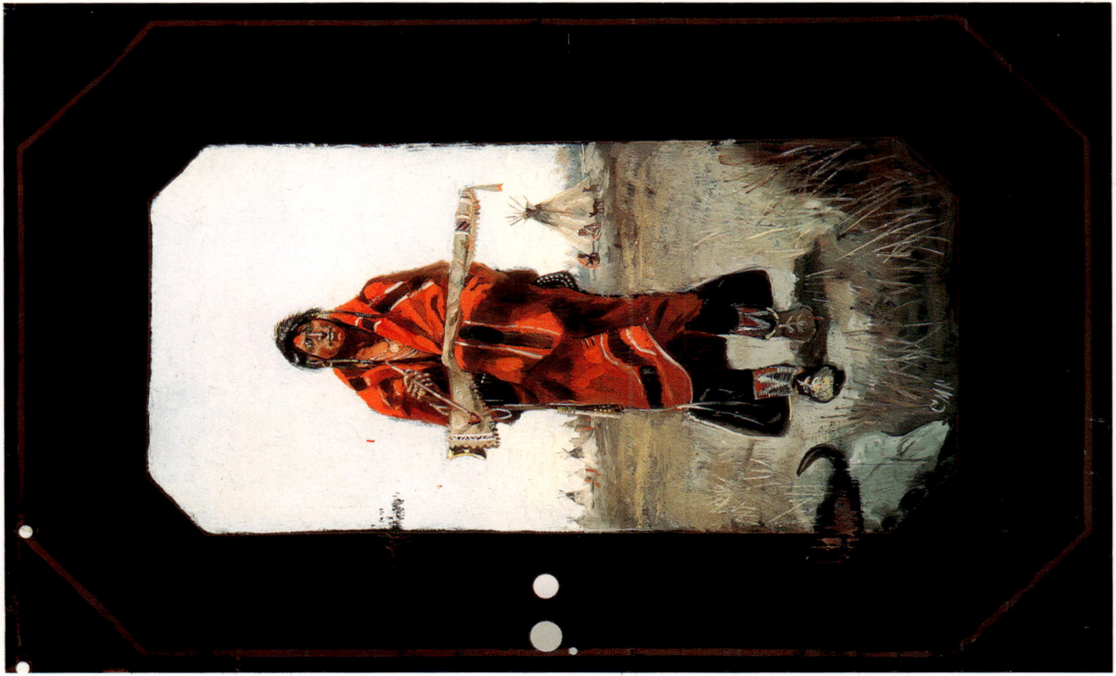

On Guard, oil on steel safe door, 1894

Russell sometimes painted his images on non-traditional surfaces like this steel safe door, as well as on mirrors, cigar boxes, and wood panels. The buffalo skull in the foreground was his trademark; it later became smaller and more simplified.

From the collection of the C. M. Russell Museum, Great Falls, MT.

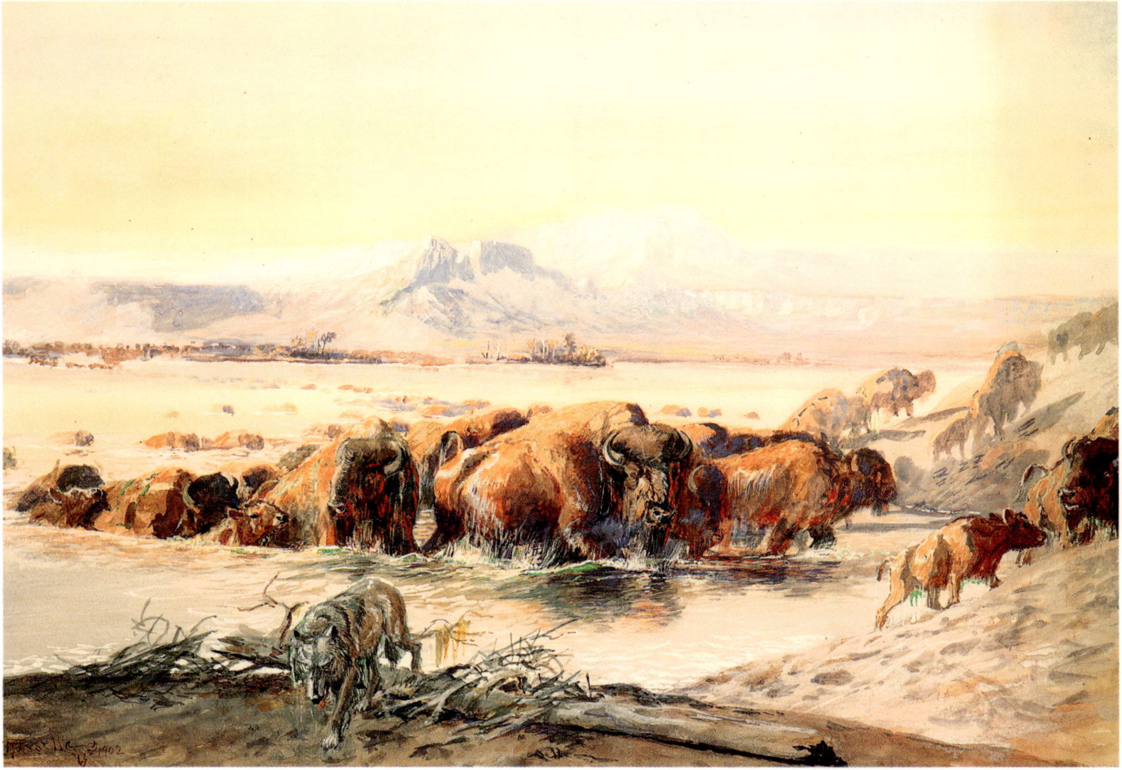

THE C.M. RUSSELL POSTCARD BOOK

The Upper Missouri in 1840, watercolor, 1902

Russell felt a powerful nostalgia for the Old West. Some of what he painted he had witnessed with his own eyes. Some–like this scene that had occurred before his birth–he heard about from Native American friends.

From the collection of the C. M. Russell Museum, Great Falls, MT.

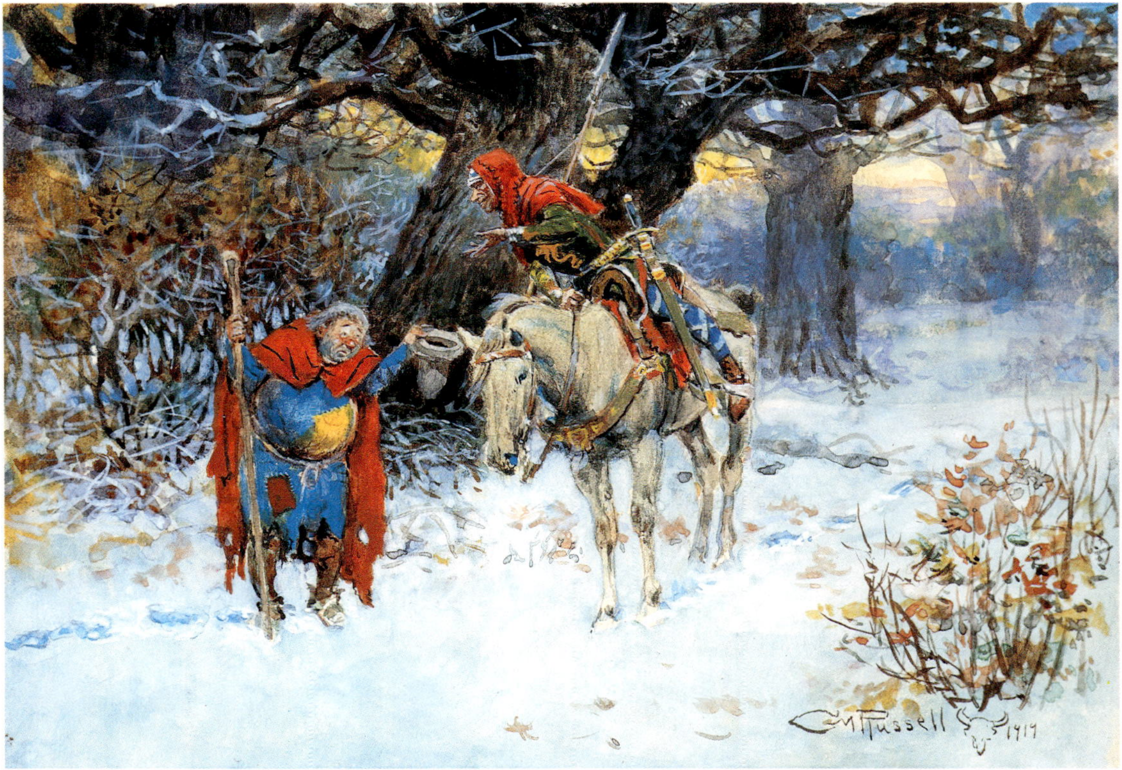
CM Russell 1919

The Fat Beggar, watercolor, 1919

From the collection of the C. M. Russell Museum, Great Falls, MT.

Though most of his subject matter was western, Russell sometimes ventured far afield, as with this English Christmas scene. Several of his paintings of English historical subjects survive.

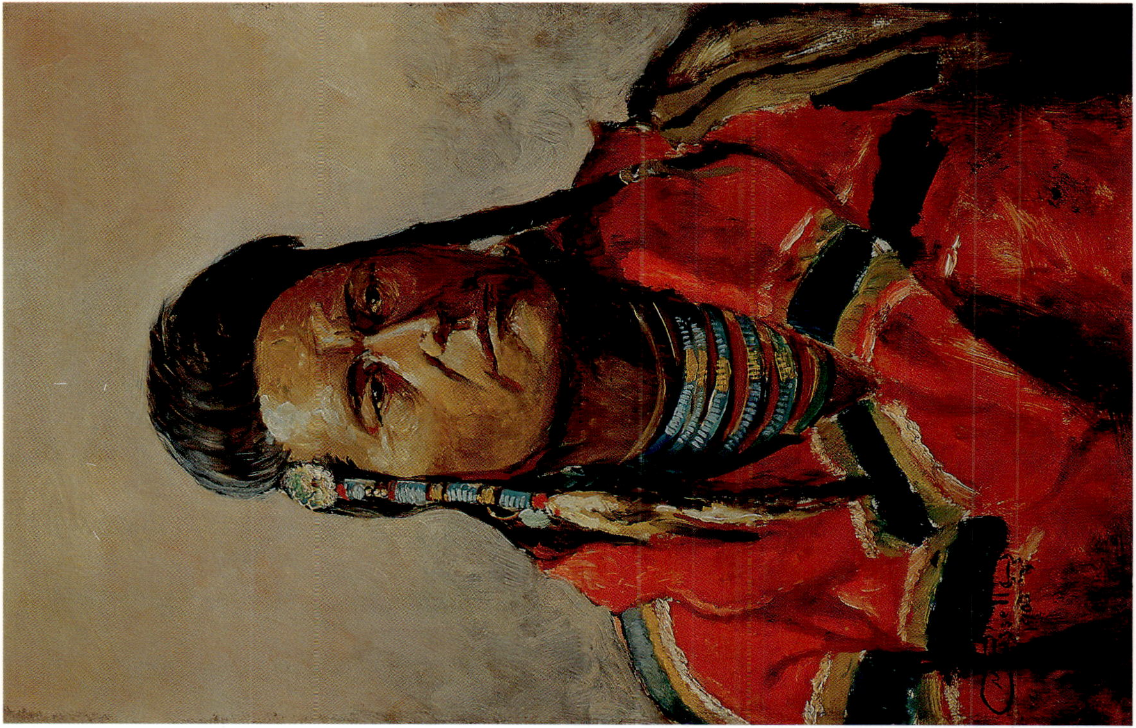

THE C.M. RUSSELL POSTCARD BOOK

Chief Joseph, oil, 1900

This portrait captures the dignity and courage of Chief Joseph, spiritual leader of the Nez Perce during their historic flight from their ancestral lands in Idaho to Montana's Bears Paw Mountains.

From the collection of the C. M. Russell Museum, Great Falls, MT.

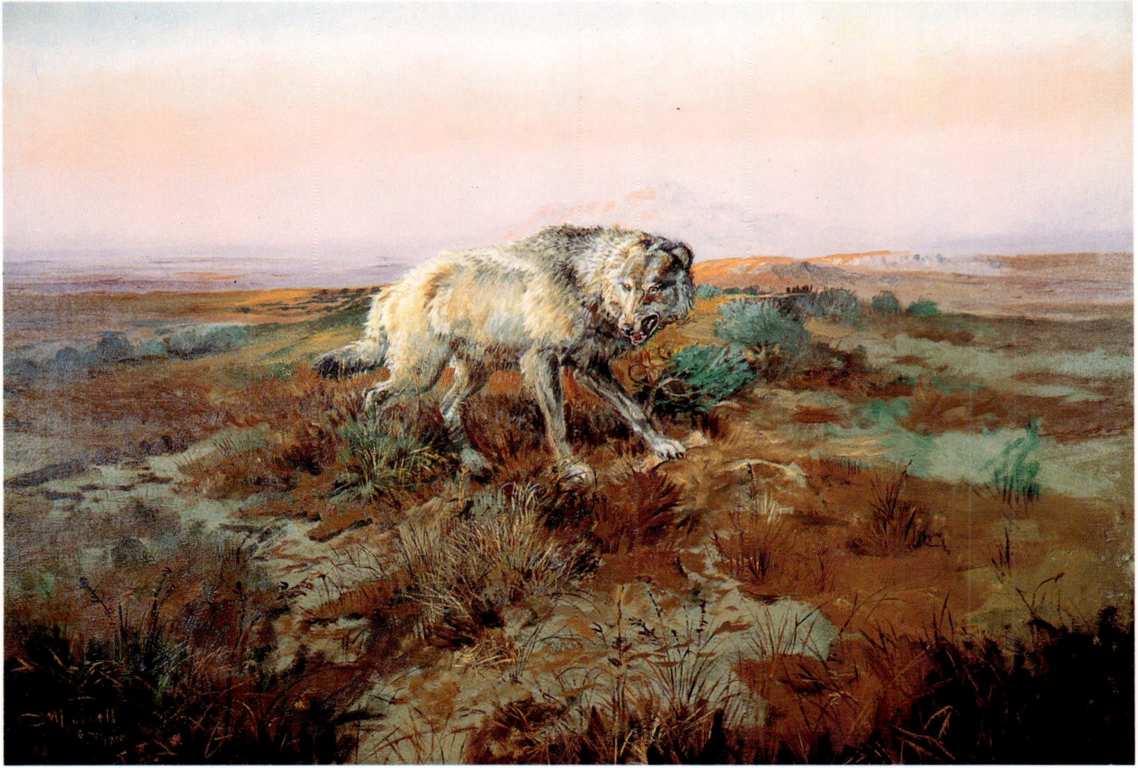

THE C.M. RUSSELL POSTCARD BOOK

Lone Wolf, oil, 1900

Wolves were not popular among the settlers of the West. Russell felt differently, and in this image, he celebrates the majesty of the wolf, one of "nature's people," as he called wild animals.

On loan to the C.M. Russell Museum, Great Falls, MT, from the Jack Hoover Collection.

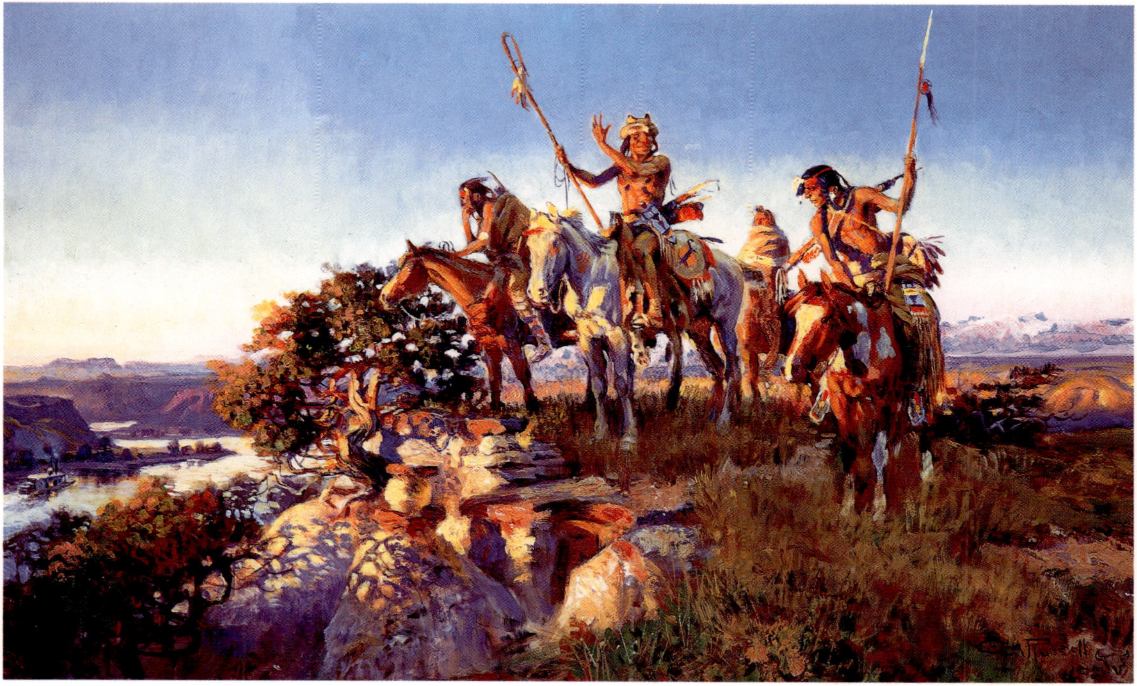

THE C.M. RUSSELL POSTCARD BOOK

The Fireboat, watercolor, 1898

A party of Native Americans is startled to see a steamboat coming up the Missouri River under its own power. In sign language, the gesture of two upraised fingers means "fire" and "water."

From the collection of the C. M. Russell Museum, Great Falls, MT.

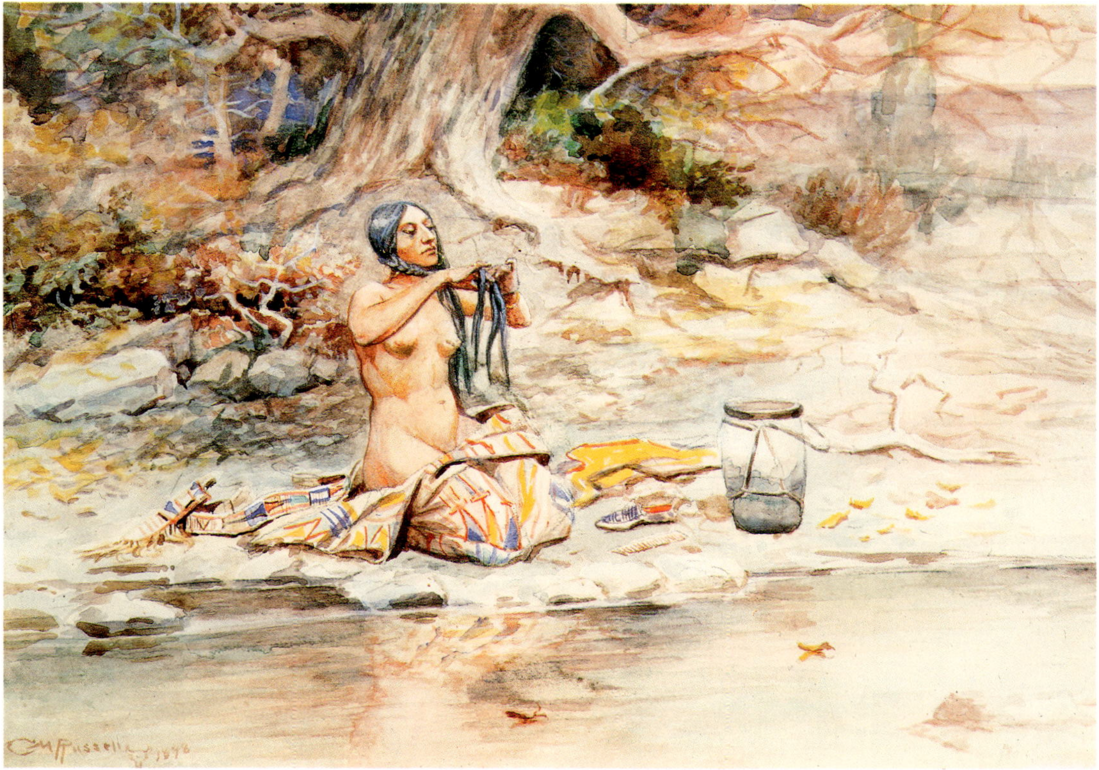

THE C.M. RUSSELL POSTCARD BOOK
Indian Maiden Braiding Her Hair, watercolor, 1898

From the collection of the C. M. Russell Museum, Great Falls, MT.

With this watercolor–an example of his mastery of the medium–
Russell offers an idyllic vision of Native American life before
it was disrupted by white "civilization."

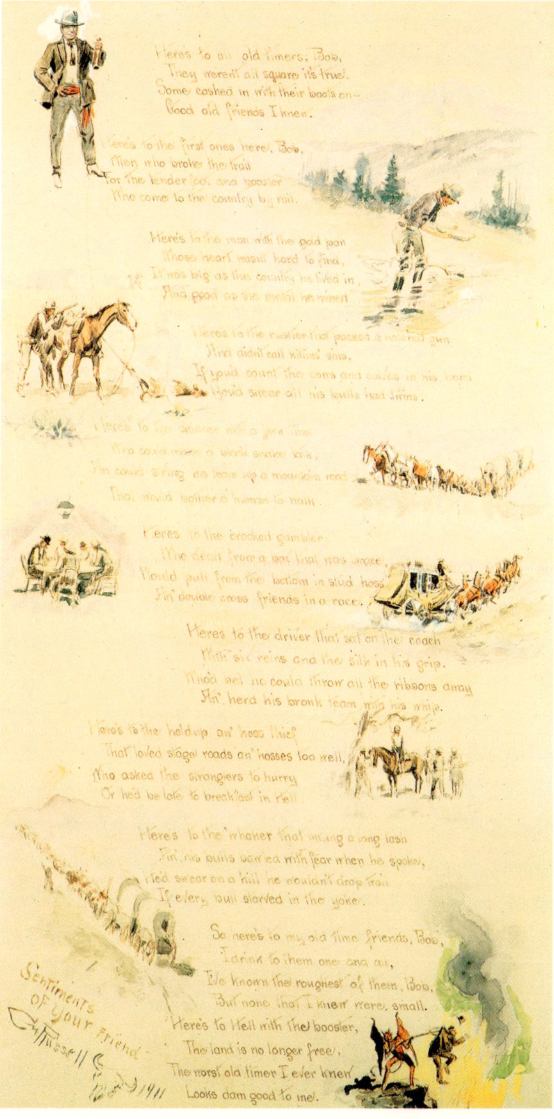
Heres to all old timers, Bob,
They werent all square its true.
Some cashed in with their boots on-
Good old friends I knew.
Heres to the first ones here, Bob,
Men who broke the trail
For the tender foot and booster
Who come to the country by rail.
Here's to the man with the gold pan
Whose heart wasnt hard to find,
It was big as the country he lived in,
And good as the metal he mined.
Heres to the rustler that packed a notched gun
And didnt call killin' sins,
If youd count the cows and calves in his herd
Youd swear all his bulls had twins.
Heres to the skinner with a jerk line
Who could make a black snake talk,
An could string his team up a mountain road
That would bother a human to walk.
Heres to the crooked gambler
Who dealt from a box that was arore,
Would pull from the bottom in stud hoss
An' double cross friends in a race.
Heres to the driver that sat on the coach
With six reins and the silk in his grip.
Whod bet he could throw all the ribbons away
An' herd his bronk team with his whip.
Heres to the holdup an' hoss thief
That loved stage roads an' hosses too well,
Who asked the strangers to hurry
Or hed be late to breakfast in Hell.
Here's to the whaner that swung a long lash
An' his bulls worried with fear when he spoke,
Hed swear on a hill he wouldnt drop trail
If every bull starved in the yoke.
So here's to my old time friends, Bob,
I drink to them one and all,
Ive known the roughest of them, Bob,
But none that I knew were small.
Here's to Hell with the booster,
The land is no longer free,
The worst old timer I ever knew
Looks dam good to me.
Sentiments of your Friend
CM Russell
1911

THE C.M. RUSSELL POSTCARD BOOK

Here's to All Old Timers, Bob, watercolor/illustrated poem, 1911

This illustrated letter honors Robert Vaughn, an old Russell friend, on his 75th birthday. The poem expresses Russell's love for the past and his affection for all its characters, good and bad.

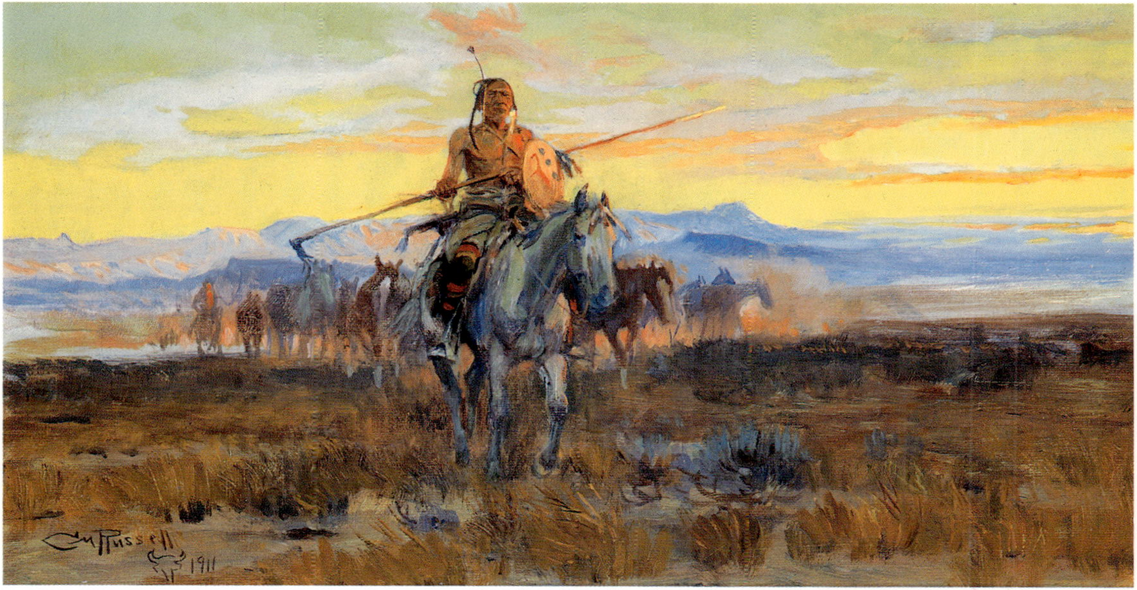
CM Russell
1911

THE C.M. RUSSELL POSTCARD BOOK
Stolen Horses, oil on board, 1911

With his rich colors and dramatic lighting, Russell recreates an earlier, simpler world, one of haunting beauty. *Stolen Horses* is a small oil, only eight by fourteen inches.

From the collection of the C. M. Russell Museum, Great Falls, MT.

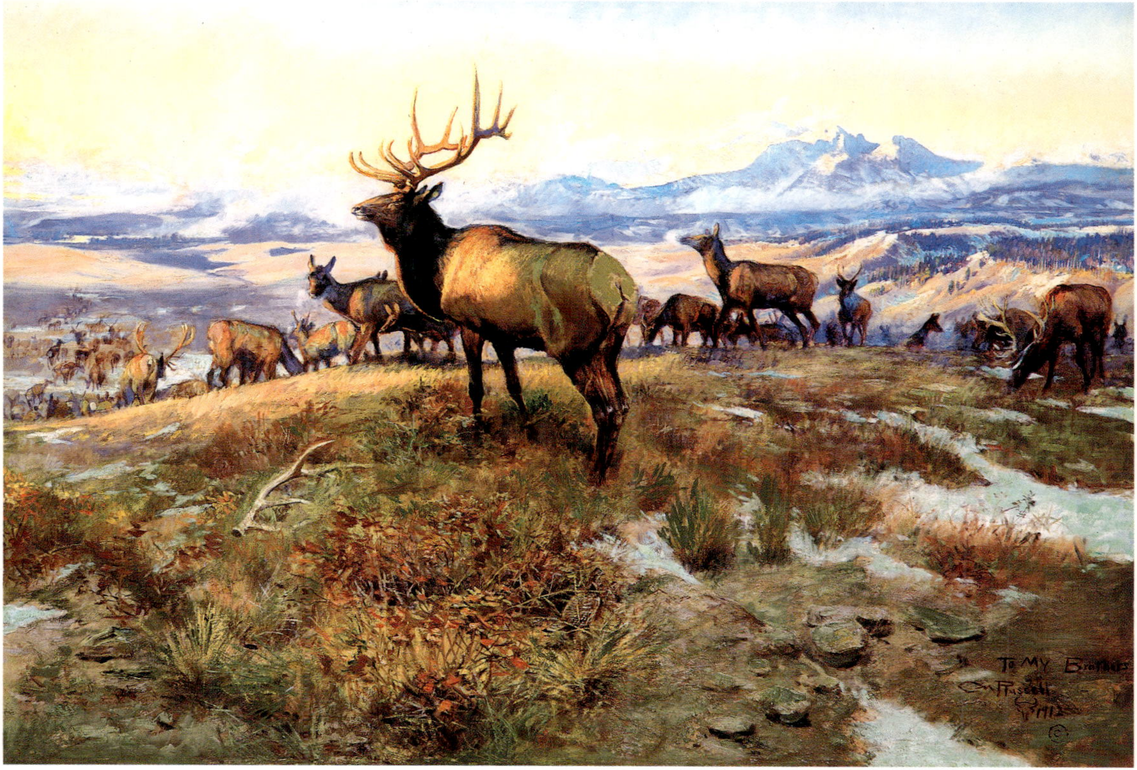
To My Brothers
CM Russell
1912
©

THE C.M. RUSSELL POSTCARD BOOK
The Exalted Ruler, oil, 1912

From the collection of the C. M. Russell Museum, Great Falls, MT.

Asked to create an artwork for the new home of the Great Falls, Montana, Elks Club, Russell promised to "paint some old thing." This magnificent painting–measuring 54"x72"– was the result.

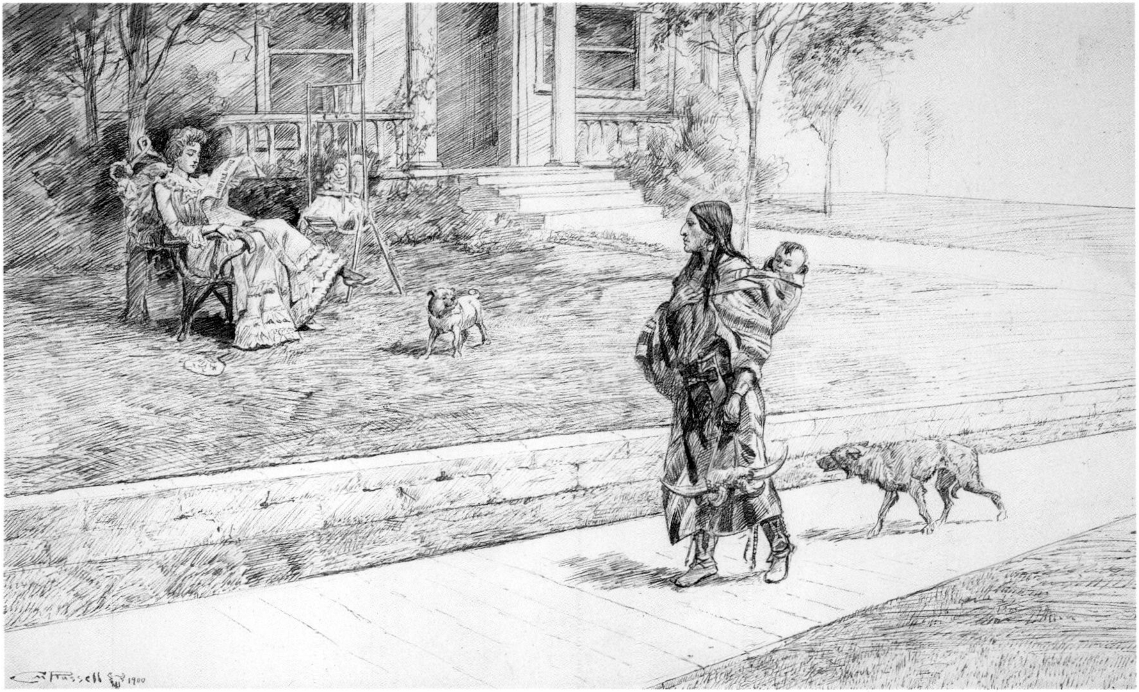
CMRussell 1900

THE C.M. RUSSELL POSTCARD BOOK

Mothers under the Skin, pen and ink, 1900

This fine example of Russell's work in pen and ink celebrates the universality of motherhood while noting the radical differences between two cultures.

From the collection of the C. M. Russell Museum, Great Falls, MT.

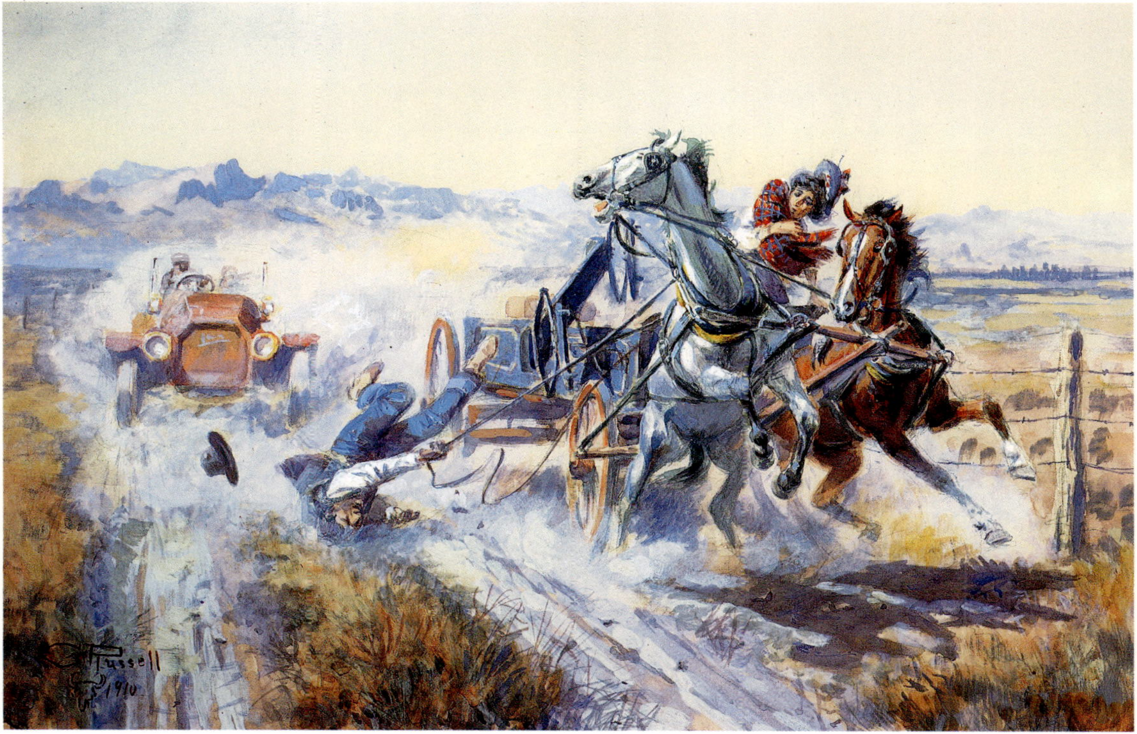
CM Russell
1910

THE C.M. RUSSELL POSTCARD BOOK

The Old Story, watercolor, 1910

Together with a painting called *The Life Saver*, *The Old Story* was an advertisement for a Minneapolis seatbelt company. At the same time, it dramatized Russell's recurrent theme of the conflict between the new and the old West.

From the collection of the C. M. Russell Museum, Great Falls, MT.

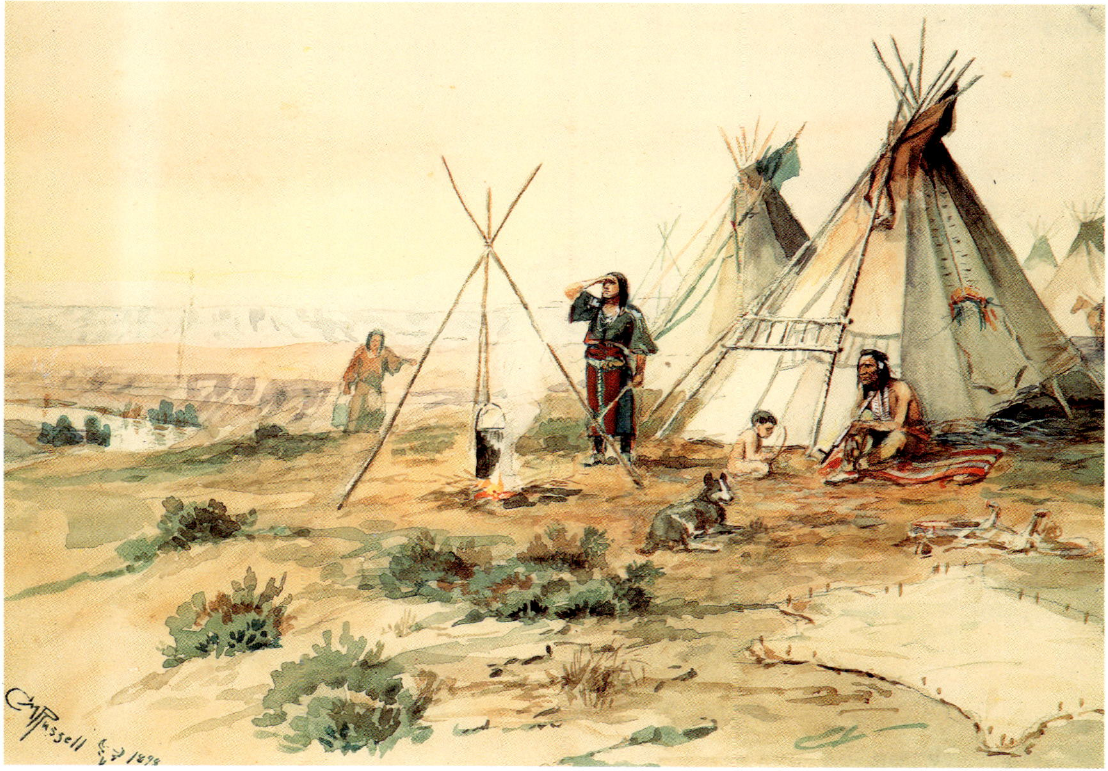
CMRussell
1898

THE C.M. RUSSELL POSTCARD BOOK
Indian Camp, watercolor, 1898

From the collection of the C. M. Russell Museum, Great Falls, MT.

One of Russell's many works on Native American subjects, this painting provides valuable information about teepee structure, cooking, and preparation of hides.

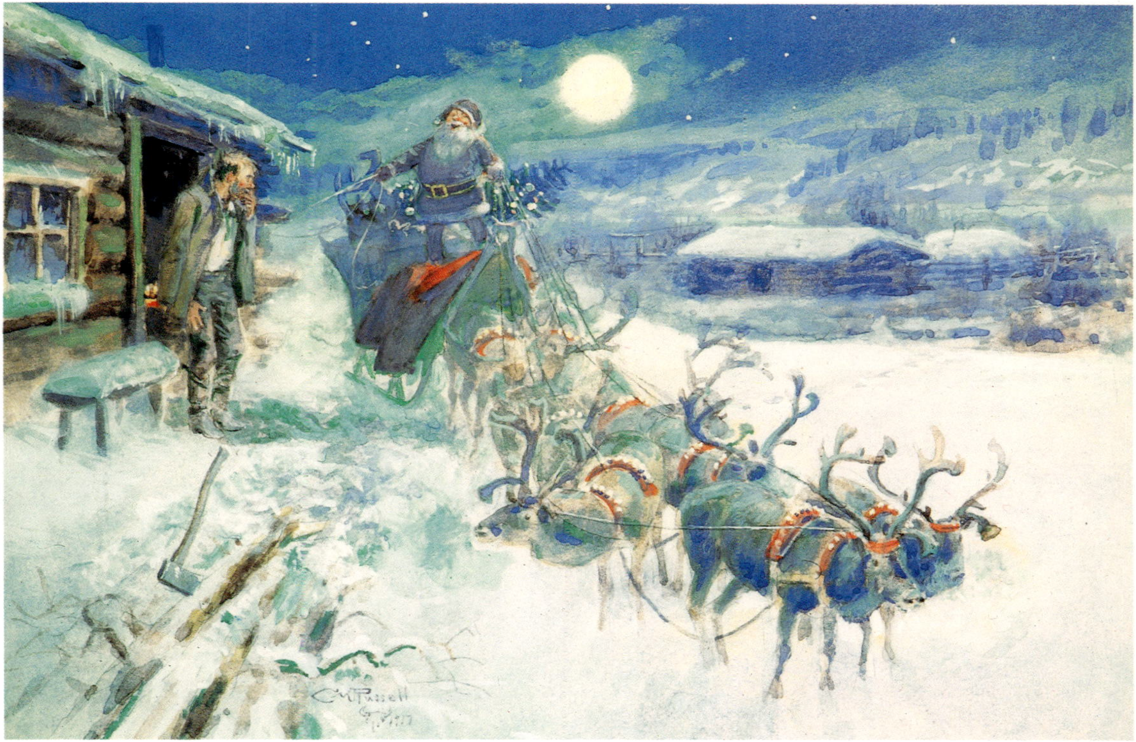
CMRussell

THE C.M. RUSSELL POSTCARD BOOK
Christmas at the Line Camp, watercolor, 1917

In the poem accompanying this Christmas painting, Russell called Santa Claus "An old time freighter I knowed before/ . . . an under sized skinner/ Good natured and stout."

From the collection of the C. M. Russell Museum, Great Falls, MT.